ADDICTION

The Superhero Lover Presents

ADDICTION

Addicted with No Conviction

Shaun Saunders

Shaun Saunders
Hampton, GA

Addiction: Addicted with No Conviction

Cover design by TLH Designs, Chicago, IL (www.lovetlhayden.com)

Book design by Kingdom Living Publishing, Accokeek, MD (www.kingdomlivingbooks.com)

For information about this book or to contact the author, send an email to:

thesuperheroteam3@gmail.com

Published by:
Shaun Saunders
Hampton, GA

Published in the United States of America.
ISBN 978-0-578-93457-0

Contents

Foreword

Addiction is a book that will take the reader on an internal journey identifying how choices have shaped our lives in our decision-making; how the amount of emotional energy we have spent entangled in unhealthy relationships have drained our time; and the inability we sometimes face trying to come to grips with who we are and becoming the person God intended. *Addiction* goes even deeper by helping us understand how the addict and the addict enabler coexist because they are the same person.

We are living in a moment where addictions of varying degrees are eroding the societal structures across our nation. And with these addictions, men seem to be the alarming statistic and diminishing figures. The relevance and timing of this book are paramount because very few men are willing to come from a place of vulnerability, sharing their pains and mishaps, to ensure another generation of men do not drift down the same path of unfulfilled aspirations, uninspired creativity, and talents remaining dormant.

Over the years that I have known Pastor Shaun (Saunders), he has emphatically expressed his desire to see the lives of men restored so they can stand with confidence in their home, community, and workplace. Countless times he has empowered men to rise from the shame of their past and live a transformative life in Christ.

Addiction will help men across all demographic spectrums to address the pain that exists and begin the healing process through personal reflection and accountability. Let the journey to wholeness begin.

"...Anyone who belongs to Christ has become a new person. The old life is gone; a new life has begun" (2 Corinthians 5:17, NLT)!

Pastor Terry Gainer

Introduction

Within the mastered mind of humanity's masked presentation of itself lies the unresolved threat of unhinged conspirators, cohabitating personalities with independent expressions deceitfully working together, split on which of their conflicted minds has the legal authority to control the vulgarly aggressive actions of their inner BEAST. Whether we deny or accept him, all of us, granted with the benefit of occupying a space of time in a realm spoiled with the freedoms of our choices, are infected with the hazardous desires of an unchained BEAST that our Creator has allowed to reside within the fragility of our bodies for which He decided to protect in the perfect innocence of His majestic mystique. The BEAST is an addict desensitized from the possibility of reconciling himself back into a right stand with his creator first, then himself second through the transformational power of a moral measuring stick called conviction. The Beast is real, and dismissing the powering presence of his existence only creates greater opportunity for him to commit acts of indecent exposure when he chooses to reveal his actions in the public eye through a lack of an intimacy we've all longed to experience in our private lives.

The transcript you are about to read is the Superhero's awkwardly suspicious statement of admission declaring in the words of R. Kelly, "I admit that I did it" captured on an audio recording retrieved from an undercover surveillance sting conducted by the Secret Services of the Superhero Lover's arch-nemesis, The Accuser of the Brethren. The details uncovered in this audio are explicit, unhindered by the redactions of outsiders determined to expel the deplorable actions of the Beast from the history of the Superhero Lover's story. WARNING: The evidence revealed within the context of this transcript will challenge you to look into the eyes of the unmastered BEAST living in you, that has unleashed itself from the once heavily manned prison managed by a jury of wavering conspirators fighting over who has the right to control his actions. It will cause you to confess up to your addiction, admit you're an addict with no conviction hindered by your suppression of madness that conflicts with your disposition.

In addition to facing the wrath of his monster, this chronicling in the Superhero saga will examine the complexity of the Superhero's transformation from an addict addicted with no conviction, into the unfathomable possibility of becoming a disciplined Man continuously challenged to say "No" to that uncontrolled lust that encouraged him to pursue after an addiction disguised in the clothed seduction of an illusion stimulated by an unrealistic desire to walk in the freedom of his fantasy absent the responsibilities of his reality.

So, without further ado, The Daily Times, in collaboration with The Superhero Lover Chronicler, present to you the Superhero Lover's transcript of an audio recording entitled: ADDICTED WITH NO CONVICTIONS!

Chapter One

Beast Mode: The Addict and the Beast

"Before you can break out of prison,
you must first realize you are locked up."

Ohhhhhhh! The unethically deceitful, but joyful shout of built-up frustration being released from his constipated bowels of mercy, ignorantly parades around the innocence of an addict, residing in the all-inclusive liberty of a free-thinking society, wrapped in the garments of sensitive skin allergic to being held to a higher level of accountability because of his expulsion of their possibly being a worthy enough suitor to challenge the unchecked desires that drive his choices. As a result, of drowning in the illogical rhythm of his unjustified rationale, swimming solo in the nuances of 21st-century philosophies that promise unrestricted freedoms while secretly masking the calculated side effects of their dysfunction, the Superhero Addict is desiring to unmask himself in the daylight, under the naïve assumption that God is required to agree with his choices because he considers them to be in alignment with his decision.

Now as an addict, addicted with no conviction, in a world invested into watching others feed the flesh of their beast with the addictive prescription they offer up as a solution only to initiate their control over the ignorant, the Superhero arrogantly walks around in the distorted perception of a God image he was naturally created to reflect. These unnatural affections, however, that ruthlessly pursue after emotional desires and not his desire for the things that God desires for him to have, have allowed his addicted beast to unworthily sit on the throne of his life, to which he has for years continued to bow himself down and pledge his allegiance to. After years of feenin for a fix and prostituting his soul, without any conviction, over to the fantasies of an unreliable pimp, he, like the prodigal son, has a coming to himself moment after recognizing he has turned into the hoe his addiction assured him he would never become.

With no physical strength to turn away from a lifelong addiction that has lived a prosperous life through a false sense of entitlement that continues to justifiably comfort him with an attitude intent on entertaining his pleasure principle through the ignorance of his dysfunction, the beast seeks to be released from the natural reflection of the God image he was supposed to reflect, in order to qualify the naturally immoral life of the distorted perception of God's idea he emotionally contends by nature, not by choice, he is. This unjustifiable perspective is a fallacy most addicts hang their hats on, hoping to expunge the impact of the role they played in the death of a mutilated soul, horrifically murdered by the freedom of their decisions. In the words of Pastor Keion Henderson, "You're born looking like your parents, but you die looking like your decision." Addiction is a choice that attacks the psychological, emotional, physical, and spiritual immune systems of the undisciplined with a contagious virus called self-righteousness illegally downloaded onto a hard drive all because of an owner incorrectly installing the security protection software program. It is a disease of isolation. As the Superhero sinks deeper and deeper into its deadly stronghold, he becomes isolated from others and himself as deeply rooted feelings of inner insufficiency and not being "enough" create the overwhelming need for an addiction that bullies him around.

As the fame of the Superhero's addiction begins to spread on the big screens of highly frequented social media outlets, the quarrel between his supporters and his haters gathers fans together into the overcrowded stadium of public opinion to voice their standing position on the newly acquired revelations involving his addiction. Strangely enough, an overwhelming show of appreciation for the coming out of his closeted addict, celebrated by audiences fooled by the deception of inclusiveness seductively immersed in the arrogant ignorance a free-spirited culture, has diagnosed the dysfunction of the Superhero's beast as an expected norm within the function of his human nature. His guilt, clearly authenticated with an abundance of evidence fueled by the documented testimony of his victims, has challenged his prosecutors with the dubious task of providing some kind of restorative plan of action for his uncontrolled beast, the beast the world continuously encourages to run around outside the restrictions of his cage without a leash. Unfortunately, the Superhero Lover, like so many others, has been prematurely exposed and pridefully enticed by the luxury of societal privilege, without the disciplining power of God to manage oneself within the restrictive walls necessary to ensure the fulfillment of God's promise for all humanity. A society without restrictive walls built to reinforce, protect, and reveal the plans of our Creator within the psychology of human morality is a world that seeks to survive on the emotions of its mischief, numb to God because it is ill-advised about the power produced by restraint.

Where there is no vision [no revelation of God and His word], the people are unrestrained; But happy and **blessed is he who keeps the law [of God]** (Proverbs 29:18, AMP).

Before exposing the true identity of his idolatrous beast, it would be in the best interest, for the purpose of clarity, to differentiate the addict from an expression wrongly accused as the cause of his addiction. So how do we distinguish the behavioral expression of an addict from the corruptibility of his inhumane beast sitting on the throne as the root cause of an addiction that chooses to reveal its rebellious attitude through the pores of the Superhero's undisciplined flesh? What is it that has his nose open wide, smelling himself with the cheap thrill of a provocative seduction that leaves him drenched in the sweat of his sins' efforts absent the fulfilling satisfaction of obtaining those rewards God destined to dwell in the power of his possession? So just what is it that has the Superhero Lover declaring, in the words of Jodeci, "I can't leave you alone; you got me feenin?"

Since his childhood, it appears that the ruthless tenacity of the Superhero's baby beast has matured by feeding off the leftovers of his submission and his perverse lust that has left him sinking in the unchartered oceans of his sin. Absent the numbness to the once innocent proclivities his cute little baby beast used to participate in, those he once ignored, the Superhero allows the weakness of his perverse addiction to overpower his strong man, out of shape due to a lack of self-discipline. So just what is the name of this sinful aggression that we, up to this point, have only identified as the ravenous BEAST cohabitating within the anatomy of the Superhero genetic makeup? No longer sheltered by the comfort of those cheap thrills that caused him to prostitute the reward of his satisfaction for the costly consequences of elusive moments that depressed his pleasure, the Superhero engages in a heatedly intense conversation with his most challenging opponent out of all his enemies, his addict more commonly referred to as "The Beast."

"I presumed you'd satisfy my pleasure, but you left me confronting the challenges of your inevitable error. You are the villain seeking to sabotage my story's history, the antagonist corrupting the integrity of my Superhero mystery. Your elusive seduction, motivated by the pleasures of contradiction, got me feenin like an addict addicted and numb to the possibility of conviction. Postured between the compromise of both my prior and current positions, I now question my existence in multiple realms of exotic dimensions. Seeking after pleasure that promised, but never satisfied, soliciting my gift like a pimp pimping his trick in front of his paying entourage. How can it be? You're a beast, aggressive like Patrick Beverly, juggling responsibilities with little to no integrity. Though I tried to erase your presence from my autonomous reality, that marked the battlefield of my soul as the space of war between two cohabitating personalities.

Your attempted assault to emasculate me from the authenticity of my masculinity has scarred my confidence, causing me to doubt if I would ever be able to perform up to the demand of God's expectation. You are an imposter, clothed with the conflicting opinions of multiple personalities cohabitating within the explanations of my thinking, each campaigning for my vote to be the governing authority of my soul. Assuming you to be the lesser of multiple evils to which I was misleadingly convinced I had to choose from, I ignorantly cast my ballot for you, the candidate that appealed most to the thorn I pleaded to God to remove from my flesh.

Your code name, Mr. Nasty Nice, or the name other heroes like myself have come to know you more intimately as, Mr. Pornography, has allowed you the comfort of slipping under the radar of my family and friends, disguised as the most reasonable alternative for me to lean on while starving for the fulfillment of Mrs. Destiny's sexual nourishment I needed to satisfy my undisciplined sexual urges. I convinced myself that my lusting eyes and my lusting heart were natural habits of instinct that needed to be pleasured with a plethora of deliciously flavored female anatomies that dangled the luxurious perfection of my fantasy over a resentment towards the Lady of My Life present with me in my reality. I aggressively observed, never touched, but thought I intimately connected with strange women that seduced me into believing they were mine and I was theirs. Your seduction, however, deceived me, causing me to sink down into a pit dug up by a devil clothed in the beautiful body of a sexy, big booty, thick thighs, and perky breasted female lioness that castrated and killed multiple men who decided it was okay for her to handcuff them to her bed of affliction. Men like me, who have been incarcerated for so long by the memory of your oily silhouette, the erotic fruit dripping from the words of your lips, and my naïve assumption that I possessed power over your body at the digression of my pleasure has caused me to snuggle my vulnerability up in the arms of devils not possessed with the power to satisfy my satisfaction.

I worshipped you in the ignorant shame of unholiness, believing you were the one thing under the management of my control that willfully obeyed me. I pursued you because, in the false notion of my insecurities, you were the one thing I could control, even if I were not in control of anything else within the shaky walls of my life. You promised me pleasures but filled the womb of my once innocent heart with the misogynist semen of your deadly sting to incubate the seeds of an unethical generation of wild beasts birthed prematurely in the belly of your under-developed and demonically possessed soil. With my permission, you forcefully penetrated the unsupervised walls of my sanity, slipping a rufie into the unguarded open container of my psychology, paralyzing my will with an inability to identify, fight off, and cast down every imagination and every high thing that exalts itself above the knowledge of God.

"The world is unprincipled. It's dog-eat-dog out there! The world doesn't fight fair. But we don't live or fight our battles that way—never have and never will. The tools of our trade aren't for marketing or

manipulation, but they are for demolishing that entire massively corrupt culture. We use our powerful God-tools for smashing warped philosophies, tearing down barriers erected against the truth of God, fitting every loose thought and emotion and impulse into the structure of life shaped by Christ. Our tools are ready at hand for clearing the ground of every obstruction and building lives of obedience into maturity" (2 Corinthians 10:5-6, MSG).

Honestly, I could go on and on for days about you, crowning you as the mastermind that influenced the duel between the cohabitating personalities warring for the privilege my body controls. The ultimate objective in your scheming ways never changes but has always been for the innocent to preoccupy the intimate moments of our time with you, by convincing us that you should be esteemed as the highest priority of our worship, within a current dimension of time only God created and designated for us to occupy. Time, however, is God's privilege to us all, not a promise. It is the distance and space between two dimensions of reality that God has designated for us to occupy, used to measure the authenticity of His reflection at the core of His creation. I cannot manage time because I do not control it. I have learned, however, that the one thing I can manage is myself within the currency of the time God allotted for me to occupy while I exist in this world. Time is a privilege that He has provided to all humankind to reveal the layers of His immutable existence for the partakers of His creation to comprehend a King's attitude of approach towards the residents residing within his Kingdom. So, if I continue following you down this road of almost no return, how will I answer God when He asks me:

"How much of myself can I reveal through you to other people about me, without you compromising the integrity of my character?"

So no, I will not allow you the honor of my concession to a claim that acknowledges you as the unconquerable obstacle the ended the destined dynasty of The Superhero Lover's journey to God success, but rather declare today that my fall from God's grace is because of me, myself, and I. I acknowledge that the illusive lust of Judas in me has opened my soul up to feast on immoral desires fueled by the instability of an illogical emotionalism. It was never you, but it has always been me. For some time now, it seems that I have always understood this to be the actual reality of every addict, addicted with no conviction of

God's truth. The truth exposed, unfortunately, in no way minimizes the selfish urges of an addicts delight to trick and treat, every now and then, because of naïve assumptions that depend on the weakness of an addict's ability to restrict oneself, when unaccompanied by a righteous discipline needed to resist those idolatrous cravings that stimulate the dysfunction of his wayward appetites.

Like a women, physically abused by the man who promised he would never lay a hand on her, now punching her in the face, damaging the beauty of her soul with the insecurities of his maleness strangely convincing her to stay connected despite the abnormality of his rage, I for reasons I can't explain have continued to rock with you all night long. Even though I know you and I are not destined partners, the exhilarating thrill of your pompous spontaneity continuously caused me to yield myself over to the never-ending promises of an affair that appealed to the unhealthy cravings of my flesh more than the only reasonable alternative capable of removing the stench of your odor downloaded onto the hard drive of my mind. Frankly, you are only here because I allowed you for years to keep coming back in. You are only and have always been a symptom existing in the fragility of my life, echoing for me the internal pains of a deeper seeded issue longing to be rescued from the most abominable prison constructed in my history, ME!

So, as an addict, just where do I run to when both the addict and the addict enabler are found cohabitating in the same house, merging the pain of the offended and heartless cowardice of the offender inside the faltering flesh of God's man better known as, ME? I acknowledge that I am standing here dressed in the sinned silk clothing of my despair because of the self-inflicted wounds that bleed uncontrollable that I carved into the anatomy of my soul with the razor-sharp knife of my own insecurities. I fooled around with you because, at first glance, you were pleasing to my eyes, attractive on the outside, but you left me with the sour after taste of the forbidden fruit that caused me to unfathomably exist in the shame of my nakedness. Even while knowing that Jesus was the only alternative through which I could legitimately overturn my addiction, the demand of Jesus' alternative appeal disinterested me because of the uncertainty in my ability to remain disciplined while committing myself to the opportunity of its potential possibility. Just how could I walk in the love of Jesus' gracious kindness but step out on my Savior to engage in a meaningless fling with a multiplicity of strange women that propositioned me continuously with multiple opportunities to exercise the reality of my fantasies? Why, in my perception, was the love relationship I have with Jesus not enough to keep me safe from the temptation of other imposturous lovers encouraging me to explore the freedoms of life's availability that exist outside of the demanding conditions of my gracious Savior's protection?

Like many other Superheroes out there struggling with some form of addiction, I ask you: Is it possible to love, have a heart for Jesus, and be an addict addicted with no conviction all at the same time? Do the Jesus Superheroes like me, present today, lack the alternative appeal that would highlight the benefits of His grace to be more reproable than the momentary pleasures of a sin that never satisfy? Are both your Jesus lover and your addict addicted with no conviction residing actively in your house all at the same time?"

Take a moment to answer the questions related to this chapter on the next page. Remember to research and cite textual evidence to support your conclusion.

1. Reread the following statements from paragraph #1 down below. Each phrase was taken from a sentence built into the context of the passage. In your own words, explain how these statements reveal the world's attitude or approach towards people struggling with addictions. How do you believe an addict could somehow come to a logical conclusion that their loved ones don't love them because of their unwillingness to accept their choices?

Statements

"…residing in the all-inclusive liberty of a free-thinking society, wrapped in the garments of sensitive skin allergic to being held to a higher level of accountability."

"Superhero Addict is desiring to unmask himself in the daylight, under the naïve assumption that God is required to agree with his choices because he considers them to be in alignment with his decision."

____

____

____

____

____

____

____

____

____

____

2. How does the author define the word "Addic-
    tion" in paragraph #3? How has your choice
    of addiction affected your emotional, physical,
    and spiritual life?

    ____

    ____

    ____

    ____

    ____

    ____

    ____

    ____

3. Give a brief description of the Superhero
    Lover's addiction, he refers to as "Beast." Now
    give a description of your addiction you would

identify as the beast influencing your choices. (Remember to call out your addiction by name.)

____

____

____

____

____

____

____

____

____

4. Based on chapter one, how would you characterize the Superhero as an addict? Give a few words to describe where he stands currently and explain why you chose those words. Do you remember going through this phase on your journey to recover from addiction? Explain.

____

____

____

____

____

____

____

____

____

____

____

5. In paragraphs #10-12, who did the Superhero ultimately come to conclude was responsible for him being an addict addicted with no conviction? Who have you come to conclude is responsible for your addiction?

____

____

____

____

____

____

____

____

____

____

6. In your opinion, is it possible for an individual to sincerely love Jesus and be an addict addicted with little to no conviction? Explain your thoughts based on your experience.

____

____

____

____

____

____

____

____

Reflection/Additional Notes

Chapter Two

The Lack of Jesus
As an Alternative Appeal

He hath no form nor comeliness; and when we shall see him, there is no beauty that we should desire him. [3] He is despised and rejected of men; a man of sorrows and acquainted with grief: and we hid as it were our faces from him; he was despised, and we esteemed him not. [4] Surely, he hath borne our griefs, and carried our sorrows: yet we did esteem him stricken, smitten of God, and afflicted (Isaiah 53:2-4, KJV).

Jesus, the name once closely associated with an intoxicating mass appeal that drew Superheroes from all generations to a spot on earth where the presence of God was an open door to heaven, has unfortunately come to be redefined under the umbrella of the world's wayward standards as a name no longer admonished in the elite realm of the sexy. At the mention of His name, every knee used to bow, but now the arrogance of the addict seeks to dismiss the contemporary relevance of Jesus' impact as a source that lacks an alternative appeal when it comes to denouncing the spell of addiction. Addiction is the consummation of the Superhero's choice that can only be nullified with a lucrative alternative that addicts perceive to be of greater value than the valuing appeal of the lust from which he or she has no desire to withdraw. Though we are informed that He had no form nor comeliness and when it came time for us to see Him, there would be no beauty that would create a desire in us for Him, His undefeated record of wins clarifies that one day every beast will bow, and every naysayer will confess that JESUS is Lord.

As the Superhero Lover ponders the credibility of his salvation because of his egregious obsession with his addiction, he seeks to hide behind the universally used and acceptable excuse of "I'm not perfect" to rationalize for his dependents an explanation of what he has not quite been able to successfully make sense of himself. Now standing in a posture of humility, he searches out to rediscover how he went from walking in the power of Jesus to soliciting his soul over to an addiction that pimped him out to multiple clients for only thirty pieces of silver. See within the eyes of Superhero Lovers and Superhero haters around the world, Jesus has been esteemed as a legend in the game, known to expose the corruption of numerous addictions that infiltrated the streets through the organized crime regimes of demonic cartels that illegally crossed over into our Kingdom borders from Gehenna (Hell). Considered the realist gangster to have ever walked the earth, Negros expeditiously moved to worship in the safety of his presence unable to be otherwise convinced that he was not the only way of escape for them from the sinking sands of their assaulting temptation.

At the beginning of the 21st century, however, the respect for the GOAT, the greatest legend of all time, Jesus, started to grow cold due largely in part to the legalization of old ideas that contradicted the principles of the Governing Kingdom Jesus revealed to free us from the regret awaiting our arrival at the end of a messed up world we discovered through self-exploration. The world's transitional toleration and acceptance of what once was wrong, now being better than alright, conspired a revolution that characterized the Jesus resistance as the misinformed as it pertains to the objectives outlined within the bylaws of his movement. As time prevailed and liberal thinkers begin rewriting the story of Jesus legendary movement to inject an acceptable context they could use as an excuse to justify the rebellion tattooed on the exterior walls of their life experience, the reigning champion became an image of the past associated with time referred to as antiquity dismissed as a source of relevance in the dumbed-down minds of modern thinkers who have no restraint.

Where there is no vision [no revelation of God and His word], the people are unrestrained; But happy and blessed is he who keeps the law [of God] (Proverbs 29:18, AMP).

While some members on the Superhero Team remained faithful to the cause, the Superhero Lover begins to question, because of his addiction, if Jesus is the one or whether he should look for another. The doubt embodied in this question became the window the Superhero left open, expecting to see his blessing slide through only to be deceived by a friendly beast that he ignorantly welcomed into his home, bent on killing, stealing, and destroying his destiny. So just how can this be? Can the Superhero Lover really love Jesus while all at the same time being an addict addicted with no conviction? Is the undisputed champion, the greatest legend of all time, Jesus, not the most suitable alternative for the Superhero, in this most critical time of his need?

While questioning his status to play the role God designated for him to play in a story God scripted, due to the horrific addiction that if left untreated could have expelled him from receiving the rewards of his Kingdom destiny, the Superhero Lover unexpectantly connects with a group of former repentant Superhero Lover addicts, changed by the sincere attraction of Jesus' caress into the epitome of a miracle he never believed he would come to see exist in the sinful flesh of mankind. Just when he was ready to give up and throw in the towel, he hears the firm footsteps of God's strongmen marching in the unity of manhood's fraternal order towards the ignorant strongholds of the immature males sin prepped addictive posture, powerfully declaring their counter-argument against the lack of Jesus as an alternative appeal with their controversial campaign slogan entitled, JESUS IS SEXY ON ME!

The JESUS IS SEXY ON ME campaign, derived from the JESUS SEXY MOVEMENT, is the original crest of a God defined manhood, pressed against the fragilely flawed flesh of saved Superheroes who have decided it would be in the best interests of addicts addicted with no conviction to be snatched out of the fire of their lust with the aggressive demonstration of transparency by a few good men willing to be vulnerable to attract the unattracted to Jesus. These Superheroes, untouched by the influences of secret societies, the fear of persecution, and the loss of followers have sacrificed the unfulfilling misguided pleasures of their addiction at an alternative altar smeared with the blood of Jesus' three degrees of separation appeal. With the one call that's all Ken Nugent approach, this tactically trained special opts team is anonymously called on to catch, extract, and restore the Superhero Lover from the misfortunes of an overwhelming addiction that conforms his lifestyle into a pattern that accommodates his beast capability of crossing over from the deceptive realms of his fantasy into the practical dimensions of his reality.

Parachuting down onto the Superhero Lover's highly addicted location, God's seal team six silently invade his constructed sanctuaries that illegally harbor historical documents, and a collection of videos downloaded in the volt of his memory chamber locked away for no other eyes, but his to see. As they move with power and precision, consciously aware that their surprise intervention would be welcomed with high levels of resistance, they violently engage their focus at all cost on the primary objective of their mission, who has to be restrained after attempting to escape from the safety of their circle. With the enemy combatants neutralized, and the Superhero Lover's addict addicted with no conviction secured, the team immediately begins to enforce the three degrees of separation debriefing withdraw process on the wounded hero, numb to the possibility of a Jesus Sexy life free from the dependence of addiction.

So just what are the three degrees of separation that saves addicts, numb to the acknowledgment of the wrong that determines the degree of their desired conviction to change? Contextually the Scriptures imply in Jude chapter one verse twenty-three for the redeemed to:

Save others, snatching them out of the fire; and on some have mercy but with fear, loathing even the clothing spotted and polluted by their shameless immoral freedom (Jude 1:23, AMP)."

The Scripture also earnestly recommend in Proverbs chapter nineteen, verses twenty and twenty-one for all Superheroes to:

Listen to counsel and accept discipline, that you may be wise the rest of your days. Many plans are in a man's heart, But the counsel of the LORD will stand (Proverbs 19:20-21, NASB).

Now as leaders transitioning into the transformational provision of the addicted addicts need at a specified moment designated within the space of his time, these once addicted, but now exonerated Superhero team members have extended a three degrees of separation safety ladder into the bottomless pit of the Superhero lovers addiction, encouraging him in his weakness to climb up out of darkness and back into the light of Jesus reflection. The first of the three degrees of separation from addiction is centered around mastering the skill of not insulting an addict with the documented allegations of their wrongs, but instead humbly positioning an addict in a corrective posture that will enable them to acknowledge the errors of their way through the lens of their own eyes. It is at this point in the Superhero Lover's intervention that the Superhero Team indirectly applies medicated treatments that eliminate the legitimate grounding of every excuse he has previously used to justify his false sense of entitlement regarding the ignorance explaining why he has earned a free pass to do whatever he wants when it comes to replacing the pains of his past with pleasures his addiction can easily provide. The old adage that speaks to the impossibility of wise counsel making change occur in people that have no desire to change is strategically dismissed from off the loaded shoulders of illegals tangled in the responsibility of what they are not responsible for, back into the court the beast of the Superhero Lover's addict that has dishonored himself by choosing not to acknowledge the discomfort associated with the guilt of his conviction.

The Superhero Lover, like all Superheroes, can only honestly gauge the integrity of his moral compass of morality when sincerely postured in a position to impartially observe how the measure of his conduct reflects the authenticity of God's character. The authenticity of God's ability to experience the full measure of His desire in the Superhero is determined by how the Superhero perceives the benefits and/or tragedy of his conduct in relation to God's demanded expectation of him. Just as the father in the story of the prodigal son refuses to echo out loud the disappointment of his son's choices, trusting God to change in his son what he had unsuccessfully attempted to change, the JESUS IS SEXY ON ME campaign's goal is to get the Superhero Lover addict to initiate his change from the perspective of a recipient affected by his addict's contribution. This act occurs at the climax of the Prodigal Son story when the son turns back towards the security of his father's safety after having a coming to himself change experience.

> *"But when he [finally] came to his senses, he said, 'How many of my father's hired men have more than enough food, while I am dying here of hunger! [18] I will get up and go to my father, and I will say to him, "Father, I have sinned against heaven and in your sight. [19] I am no longer worthy to be called your son; [just] treat me like one of your hired men."' [20] So he got up and came to his father. But while he was still a long way off, his father saw him and was moved with compassion for him and ran and embraced him and kissed him. [21] And the son said to him, 'Father, I have sinned against heaven and in your sight; I am no longer worthy to be called your son.' [22] But the father said to his servants, 'Quickly bring out the best robe [for the guest of honor] and put it on him; and give him a ring for his hand, and sandals for his feet. [23] And bring the fattened calf and slaughter it and let us [invite everyone and] feast and celebrate; [24] for this son of mine was [as good as] dead and is alive again; he was lost and has been found.' So, they began to celebrate (Luke 15: 17-24, AMP).*

When an addict, like the prodigal son, comes to their senses, it is then and only then that the possibility of change can become a reality through the power of conviction's influence. This degree of honesty within oneself is only possible through the transparent counsel of former addicts changed after encountering the immutability of Jesus while shamelessly basking in the tragedy of their weakness. It is the honesty of an admired Superhero's transparency that establishes the conditions by which the Superhero Lover must willingly come to abide in order to expose himself when in violation of a standard all the occupants privileged to be on the team are expected to uphold. Assisting with this dimension of change is the most difficult component of withdrawal, the second degree of separation, better known as the comfort of vulnerability through the honesty of transparency.

In this dimension of an addict's conflicted reality, the heights of unimaginable success to which his Superhero could possibly prevail must coincide with the level of his comfort when exposing the details of his consecutive screw ups outlined on the timeline of his life failures. It is imperative for current and prospective Superheroes to understand that the recipients of your hero's contributions will never be able to appreciate the authenticity of your success if you are never ever exposing them at some point in time to the truths behind the reality of your failures. The success of every Jesus saved Superhero, once addicted with no conviction, is revealed in his willingness to display an unusual comfort within himself that exposes the extended depths of God's reach to touch him at the weakest point of his vulnerability. This allows the hero to identify with the extended depths God was willing to reach down to rescue him from hell and the upward journey he needed to travel to elevate him to the highest levels of his heavenly success. The impact of Jesus' alternative appeal at this point echoes through the testimony of the Superhero addict's temptation, a transparency that triggers conviction in the hearts of others that Jesus is a redeemer.

On January 2, 2020, episode two exploring the tragedy of R&B superstar, R. Kelly's demise entitled Surviving R. Kelly (Part Two): The Reckoning aired on national television. With the utmost respect for the victims shackled by the oppressive seduction of the misogynistic manipulation conspired by Mr. Kelly and his enablers, I am focusing the integrity of my comments primarily on the terror of an untamed beast running the streets without checks and balances. As many tuned in to criticize either the offender or the offended, most of the people watching mistook R. Kelly's addictive dysfunction as a rarity instead of a commonality that sheds its skin differently through all the pores of humanities sinful flesh. The tendency to prioritize one's addiction above another opens illegal channels for the Beast to freely exist in a reality conditioned to support the desires of his existence. Remember, the infatuation with the strength of another man's beast that triggers his demise is the smoking mirror that causes us to neglect the Beast that appears through our addictions to whom we assist with setting the traps that snare us in the tragedy of our own failures. Like anyone diagnosed with a sickness, ignorantly medicated with the unhealthy celebration of another individual's inevitable catastrophe, the infatuation with the evil working in another will either be a comfort of contentment in the lust of a Superhero's transgression or the inspiration to flee from the poisonous bite of an arrogant beast that the Superhero refuses to affiliate himself with.

This comfort awarded in the weakness of one's vulnerability is in no way a license for the addict to normalize the symptoms of his dysfunction, but rather an acknowledged acceptance of one's own personal responsibility in choosing to have an affair on God with an adulterous companion wrapped in the mass appeal of an unfruitful obsession. Unfortunately, the Beast that escaped through the innocent adolescence of

Robert Sylvester Kelly's unaddressed childhood molestation for over thirty years has surfaced in the modern-day formality of a pied piper, instigated by the ignorance of his enablers and the shallowness of the security centered around his victims that aggressively condoned his existence. These kinds of ailments disengage the addict from the simultaneous existence of the Superhero he portrays himself to be in the eyes of an audience attracted to his appeal, without the buy-in of the transparency needed to authorize the integrity of his presentation. Transparency is a sign of the easy security through which one has humbly accepted their responsibility and the comfort with which they can openly discuss the details of their participation at the most explicit depths of their involvement in the problem to model for others the beauty of deliverance on the other side of following Jesus.

Coming to an understanding of himself while standing in the bloody misery of his vulnerability, the Superhero's addict is now comfortable enough to be transparent with outsiders about his addiction convincingly recommending Jesus as the only alternative pathway to redemption. Now the Superhero is ready to enter the last dimensioned degree of separation called the disciplinary process of withdrawing. The continuous pursuit after an addiction high doesn't come to a standstill when an addiction is called out but instead incites the Superhero to higher levels of aggression to counter the depths of its transparency. Freeing the Superhero Lover for the instinctive habits cultivated by addiction is a process that takes time, i.e., prioritizing addiction as a symptom and not the highest pinnacle of his destiny.

Saying no to what he has surrendered himself to easily say yes to is the most daunting task of withdrawing that can only be achieved with a disciplined regiment prescribed specifically for the Superhero to resist his desire to feed again on his addiction. Esteeming the value of the unknowns of a disciplined life he is unfamiliar with, over the valued pleasure of an addiction he enjoys, can only happen through a spiritually disciplined lifestyle known as fasting. Within the walled truths of Scripture, Matthew 17:19-21 reveals the strategic need for fasting to drive out the evil of the beast.

[19] Then the disciples came to Jesus privately and said, "Why could we not cast it out?" [20] So Jesus said to them, "Because of your unbelief; for assuredly, I say to you, if you have faith as a mustard seed, you will say to this mountain, 'Move from here to there,' and it will move; and nothing will be impossible for

you. ²¹'However, this kind does not go out except by prayer and fasting (Matthew 17:19-21, KJV).

Fasting is the daily feeding on every word of God while denying the gluttonous appetite to feast on the bread by which God declared man shall not live by bread alone. Fasting is the table that God has prepared for the Superhero to sit down in the presence of his enemies and be served with a cup running over with all the goodness and mercy that will follow him all the days of his life. It is the process of maturing the appetite of the greater He that is in me, while casting down the imagination and every high thing that exalts itself above the knowledge of God, and taking captive every rebellious thought working through the un-healthy cravings of the addict that is in the world to the obedience of Christ.

It is through this process the Superhero Lover comes to rediscover that fasting is not a recommended sacrifice that makes you more holy, righteous, and/or flawlessly perfect. Superheroes don't fast to become, but they fast to mature in the identity of the destined individual God has been anxiously waiting to show the world they are. Righteous Superheroes fast because that is just what righteous Superheroes do. This is not the self-righteousness of an untrained beast prematurely exposed to the thrill of temptation he was not mature enough to handle the responsibility of, but a God righteousness committed to the work of surrendering their will over to the greater will of God. Jesus models this attitude of approach towards His help in Matthew 26:39: And He went a little beyond them, and fell on His face and prayed, saying, "My Father, if it is possible, let this cup pass from Me; yet not as I will, but as You will."

The three degrees of separation mentioned above can only be calculated as guarantees when synonymously integrated into the life of an addict desiring to change. An addict, addicted with no conviction, is an oxymoron I used to reveal how Superheroes can willingly evade the integrity of their moral compass to delight in the pleasures of an addiction that causes them to forfeit an eternal satisfaction of intimacy they desire to experience only in the presence of God. Conviction is an internal cry for help that everyone feels and hears, longing for someone to come rescue heroes from an obstacle they are afraid they can't overcome. If no one ever comes to the aid of the convicted, then a numbness sets in that disregards the discretion of God's desired will for the soul, creating the opportunity for the evil within to feast on the flesh through an addiction that preoccupies the body with a never-ending pursuit after its deception.

I understand this to be true. Like the Superhero, I have struggled with addiction while saved and filled with the Holy Ghost. I know what it means to be an addict, addicted with no conviction because I lived it. My addiction was pornography. For years porn pimped me around the fantasy of its exotic world, convincing me that I was in control. I came to find out, however, that was not true. I share this with you to inform you that you are not alone. Don't allow your addiction to isolate you from God. These are the steps I have taken, and have continued to take every day, to walk in my deliverance. Draw closer to God so that you can rediscover the Power of the Superhero God wants to reveal to the world through you. I leave you with this question: How much of God's self can He reveal through you to other Superheroes about Himself without you compromising the integrity of His character?

You are God's Superhero! Let Him use you. The world is waiting for you!

Take a moment to answer the questions below that are related to this chapter. Remember to research and cite textual evidence to support your conclusion.

1. How do you think addiction distorts your perception of God's existence within the reality of your life experience?

____

____

____

____

____

____

____

____

2. How much of God's self can He reveal through you to other Superhero addicts about Himself without you compromising the integrity of His character? Explain

____

____

____

____

____

____

____

____

____

____

3. List the names of the people you seek counsel from to help with your recovery from addiction. Give a short description of how each person on your list would help you recover. Are you currently seeking advice from these individuals? If not explain why.

____

____

____

____

____

____

____

____

____

4. Write down your understanding of the three degrees of separation on the lines below. Explain how you would implement each degree of separation in the framework of your recovery plan.

____

____

____

____

____

____

____

____

____

<u>First Degree of Separation:</u> *The skill of not insulting an addict with the documented allegations of their wrongs, but rather humbly positioning an addict in a corrective posture that will enable them to acknowledge the errors of their way through the lens of their own eyes.*

____

____

____

____

<u>Second Degree of Separation</u>: *The comfort of vulnerability through the honesty of transparency.*

<u>Third Degree of Separation:</u> *The disciplinary process of withdrawing.*

5. On the lines below, write down a detail fasting plan for yourself. Remember fasting must become a part of your life. Write down your fasting regiment (whole fast, partial fast), fasting days throughout the week, Scriptures you will feed on, and the specific areas in your life you desire for God to mature you.

Other Books by the Author

The Superhero Chronicles

The Wounded Leader
(ISBN 978-0-615-65497-3)

The Superhero's Tell All Exclusive Interview
(ISBN 978-0-692-02244-3)

The Superhero Lover
(ISBN 978-0-692-77960-6)

2 Love Her No More!
ISBN 978-0-578-47952-1

Available from the author, in retail stores, on www.amazon.com and www.barnesandnoble.com, and wherever books are sold.

Contact Information

To inquire about Pastor Shaun Saunders speaking, ministering, or doing book signings and discussions at your event, you may contact him by sending an email to:

thesuperheroteam3@gmail.com

Connect with him on Twitter:

@thesuperheroteam3